Paths to Recovery Workbook

A Companion for Studying Al-Anon's Steps, Traditions, and Concepts

Al-Anon Family Groups
Help and hope for families and friends of alcoholics

Preamble

THE AL-ANON FAMILY GROUPS are a fellowship of relatives and friends of alcoholics who share their experience, strength, and hope in order to solve their common problems. We believe alcoholism is a family illness and that changed attitudes can aid recovery.

Al-Anon is not allied with any sect, denomination, political entity, organization, or institution; does not engage in any controversy; neither endorses nor opposes any cause. There are no dues for membership. Al-Anon is self-supporting through its own voluntary contributions.

Al-Anon has but one purpose: to help families of alcoholics. We do this by practicing the Twelve Steps, by welcoming and giving comfort to families of alcoholics, and by giving understanding and encouragement to the alcoholic.

—Suggested Al-Anon Preamble to the Twelve Steps

For information and catalog of literature write
World Service Office for Al-Anon and Alateen:
Al-Anon Family Group Headquarters, Inc.
1600 Corporate Landing Parkway, Virginia Beach, VA 23454-5617
Phone: (757) 563-1600 Fax: (757) 563-1656
Web site: al-anon.org/members   E-mail: wso@al-anon.org
© Al-Anon Family Group Headquarters, Inc. 2017

Al-Anon/Alateen is supported by members' voluntary contributions and from the sale of our Conference Approved Literature.

ISBN 978-0-9963064-4-7

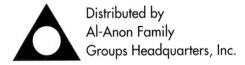

Distributed by
Al-Anon Family
Groups Headquarters, Inc.

Contents

Preface

Paths to Recovery—Al-Anon's Steps, Traditions, and Concepts (B-24) was introduced in 1997. Since that time, this in-depth study of our fellowship's three Legacies has provided Al-Anon members and groups throughout the world with an ever-increasing understanding of our fundamental principles.

Drawn from the experience, strength, and hope of hundreds of Al-Anon members, *Paths to Recovery* presents a detailed description of each of the Twelve Steps, Traditions, and Concepts of Service, with guidelines and suggestions for how to apply them to our lives. This is followed by several personal stories from members, and a series of thought-provoking questions for personal and group use.

This companion piece, the *Paths to Recovery Workbook*, contains all of the questions from the book, as well as space to answer them. It is intended not only as a convenience, but also as an additional tool for growth. Several of the Steps encourage us to express ourselves in writing. Although it is certainly beneficial to read and talk about the questions, many of us have found that writing out our answers further clarifies our thoughts, helping us to be more fully honest with ourselves. In addition, as time progresses, what we write can provide us with an extra bonus—it becomes a documented history of our own growth, by which we can more easily measure our progress.

As a member shared in *Paths to Recovery*, "The Steps show me how to love myself, the Traditions show me how to love others, and the Concepts show me how to love the world I live in." As you make use of the *Paths to Recovery Workbook*, may the love of the program grow in you "One Day at a Time."

Al-Anon's Declaration

Let It Begin with Me

When anyone, anywhere, reaches out for help,

let the hand of Al-Anon and Alateen

always be there, and—*Let It Begin with Me.*

Twelve Steps

STUDY OF these Steps is essential to progress in the Al-Anon program. The principles they embody are universal, applicable to everyone, whatever his personal creed. In Al-Anon, we strive for an ever-deeper understanding of these Steps, and pray for the wisdom to apply them to our lives.

1. We admitted we were powerless over alcohol—that our lives had become unmanageable.

2. Came to believe that a Power greater than ourselves could restore us to sanity.

3. Made a decision to turn our will and our lives over to the care of God *as we understood Him.*

4. Made a searching and fearless moral inventory of ourselves.

5. Admitted to God, to ourselves and to another human being the exact nature of our wrongs.

6. Were entirely ready to have God remove all these defects of character.

7. Humbly asked Him to remove our shortcomings.

8. Made a list of all persons we had harmed, and became willing to make amends to them all.

9. Made direct amends to such people wherever possible, except when to do so would injure them or others.

10. Continued to take personal inventory and when we were wrong promptly admitted it.

11. Sought through prayer and meditation to improve our conscious contact with God *as we understood Him*, praying only for knowledge of His will for us and the power to carry that out.

12. Having had a spiritual awakening as the result of these steps, we tried to carry this message to others, and to practice these principles in all our affairs.

Working Step One

We admitted we were powerless over alcohol—that our lives had become unmanageable.

EACH OF US is free to create our own solutions using the experience, strength, and hope of those who have gone before us. The following questions for self-study or group study may help you with Step One. As you work each Step, remember to appreciate yourself for the effort. Call a friend or Sponsor and share your success, too.

1. Do I accept that I cannot control another person's drinking? Another person's behavior?

2. How do I recognize that the alcoholic is an individual with habits, characteristics, and ways of reacting to daily happenings that are different from mine?

3. Do I accept that alcoholism is a disease? How does that change how I deal with a drinker?

4. How have I tried to change others in my life? What were the consequences?

5. What means have I used to get what I want and need? What might work better to get my needs met?

6. How do I feel when the alcoholic refuses to be and do what I want? How do I respond?

7. What would happen if I stopped trying to change the alcoholic or anyone else?

8. How can I let go of others' problems instead of trying to solve them?

9. Am I looking for a quick fix to my problems? Is there one?

10. In what situations do I feel excessive responsibility for other people?

11. In what situations do I feel shame or embarrassment for someone else's behavior?

12. What brought me into Al-Anon? What did I hope to gain at that time? How have my expectations changed?

13. Who has expressed concern about my behavior? My health? My children? Give examples.

14. How do I know when my life is unmanageable?

15. How have I sought approval and affirmation from others?

16. Do I say "yes" when I want to say "no"? What happens to my ability to manage my life when I do this?

17. Do I take care of others easily, but find it difficult to care for myself?

18. How do I feel when life is going smoothly? Do I continually anticipate problems? Do I feel more alive in the midst of a crisis?

19. How well do I take care of myself?

20. How do I feel when I am alone?

21. What is the difference between pity and love?

22. Am I attracted to alcoholics and other people who seem to need me to fix them? How have I tried to fix them?

23. Do I trust my own feelings? Do I know what they are?

Working Step Two

Came to believe a Power greater than ourselves could restore us to sanity.

THE FOLLOWING questions may assist us, individually and in our groups, to developing an understanding of the relationship of a Higher Power to our lives.

1. What is my concept of a Higher Power at this time?

2. What would it take to allow my concept of my Higher Power to change?

3. Have past experiences affected my concept of a Higher Power? If so, how?

4. What do I hope to gain from accepting the concept of a Power greater than myself?

5. Do I sense spiritual guidance in my life? How?

6. How do I describe the Higher Power I found in Al-Anon?

7. What does "Let Go and Let God" mean to me?

8. What does faith mean to me?

9. With whom and in what circumstances am I comfortable discussing my spiritual experiences?

10. What might I gain from believing I could be supported and loved by a Power greater than myself?

11. What does "Came to believe" mean to me?

12. What does sanity mean to me?

13. How has the alcoholic situation affected my sanity? My life?

14. Have I allowed the alcoholic situation to become my Higher Power? How?

15. How has my thinking become distorted trying to handle the alcoholic behavior?

16. How have I turned to a Power greater than myself in times of great need? Did I call another Al-Anon member? My Sponsor? Did I read Al-Anon Conference Approved Literature (CAL)? Did I go to a meeting? If not, why not?

17. In working this Step, can I describe a Step Two experience to my Sponsor or my group? In a written sharing?

18. When have I done the same things over and over, yet expected different results?

Working Step Three

Made a decision to turn our will and our lives over to the care of God as we understood Him.

HERE ARE some ideas and questions to ask ourselves or discuss in our group to begin exploring our relationship to the God of our understanding.

1. How do I feel about turning my life over to a Higher Power for guidance?

2. How do I know who or what my Higher Power is?

3. Am I willing to try to turn my problems over? What could help me to be willing?

4. How can I stop thinking, trying, and considering, and actually make a decision?

5. Have I had a problem making decisions in my life? Give examples.

6. If I am unable to make this decision, what holds me back?

7. Do I trust my Higher Power to care for me?

8. How might Step Three help me keep my hands off situations created by others?

9. What consequences have I had by obsessing on problems and other people?

10. When I "Let Go and Let God" take care of my life, am I willing to follow the guidance I receive?

11. How can I turn a situation over and let go of the results?

12. How can I stop myself from taking my will back?

13. What can I do when my loved ones make decisions I don't like?

14. How can I let my loved ones find their own life paths as I am finding mine?

15. What can I do to try to see others as God sees them?

16. How can I express God's will in my actions and words toward others, including the alcoholic?

Working Step Four

Made a searching and fearless moral inventory of ourselves.

AS WE BEGIN to consider the questions below, we need to remember to keep it simple and pray for guidance and courage. The following are not all-inclusive, but rather point to a beginning.

IN PREPARING TO TAKE AN INVENTORY

1.   Am I willing to look honestly at myself? What stands in my way?

2.   Have I sought help from my Higher Power, my Sponsor, or other Al-Anon members?

3.   What suggestions have I tried to see if they might work?

4.   Do I understand the spiritual principle of an inventory?

5.   What do "searching" and "fearless" mean to me?

6.   What does a "moral inventory" mean?

WE CONTINUE BY EXAMINING OUR ASSETS

AN INVENTORY is not just our faults; we must also assess our positive traits and accomplishments. If we are stymied by this task, it can be useful to think about qualities we like in others and whether we may possess that same trait.

1. In what ways am I caring? How do I empathize with other people? Am I kind to myself? Am I kind to the elderly? Children? My family? My friends? Those in need of my assistance? Am I agreeable and courteous?

2. How am I tolerant?

3. Am I open to another's point of view?

4. Do I listen in meetings and accept that others have needs different from mine?

5. Do I practice patience with a newcomer?

6. How am I trustworthy? Do I pay my bills? Am I prompt? Do I fulfill my commitments? Do I act responsible in my job? How much can my family and friends depend on me?

7. How am I honest? Do I tell the whole truth? If not, what stops me from telling the truth?

8. In what ways do I take care of myself? Do I make needed medical appointments? Do I dress appropriately? Do I eat healthy foods? Exercise? Meditate?

9. How am I respectful? Do I take care of material things, whether mine or others? Do I show respect for the law?

10. How am I generous? Do I contribute to my group? To the World Service Office quarterly appeal? Have I contributed by volunteering to be a trusted servant?

11. In what ways do I look for the good in others?

12. How am I kind? Am I considerate of other people? Do I listen patiently to a friend in need? Do I offer help when asked? Do I think to point out the good in others?

13. How do I open myself up to others?

14. How am I practical? Do I have a budget? How often do I recognize what needs to be done and then do my share?

15. How am I dependable? How often do I meet work deadlines? Do I organize well and carry out what I decide to do?

16. What are my talents? Do I have any artistic gifts? Do I beautify my surroundings? Do I have mechanical skills?

17. Do I make friends easily? Why or why not?

18. Do I have trouble with intimate relationships? Why or why not?

19. In what ways do I express myself clearly and concisely?

20. How do I see the humor in life and express it?

21. How am I optimistic?

22. How do I practice my faith in a Higher Power? In myself? In others? How do I share my faith? Do I have an attitude of gratitude?

23. How am I humble? Do I ask God for guidance and follow it to the best of my ability? When have I allowed others to share their wisdom with me? Do I ever admit mistakes? How patient am I with myself?

We now should have a list of good qualities to fortify us for the rest of the inventory. With each and every good quality we surveyed, we may have considered a quality we find uncomfortable to acknowledge. A thorough inventory, as we stated in the beginning of this chapter, includes our positive as well as negative behaviors and thoughts.

WE CONTINUE BY EXAMINING OUR LIABILITIES

NOW OUR task is to deal with the difficult issues of our lives, past and present. Nothing will be solved by hiding from the truth. Justifying and rationalizing our actions and blaming others for all the problems in our lives will never produce serenity. Remember, we are only asked to take an inventory, not to do anything about what we learn. If we trust in our Higher Power and the guidance of our Sponsor, these issues will be dealt with in a loving way as we continue to work the Al-Anon program of recovery.

1. In what ways am I resentful? Do I harbor grudges? Why?

2. Whom do I resent from my past? Why? What is my part in it?

3. Whom do I resent in my immediate environment? Why? What is my part in it?

4. Do I resent authority figures? Why? What is my part in it?

5. Do I resent places or things? Why? What is my part in it?

6. When do I judge other people harshly and resent their not doing what I think they should?

7. Do I hold everyone and everything to an impossible standard of ideal perfection?

8. How do I judge myself?

9. Am I fearful? What do I fear? Why?

10. Am I dishonest? Am I holding secrets? Do I lie rather than "cause a scene"? What dishonesty have I hidden from others?

11. Do I feel sorry for myself? Am I filled with self-pity? How do I feel I have been a victim? What is my part in it?

12. Am I a fixer? Do I like to be in charge? Do I get upset when I don't win? What consequences have I had from taking care of others instead of myself?

13. In what ways do I trust myself in dealing with others? Do I go to safe places? Do I remove myself from potentially dangerous situations? Even if it's my own home?

14. In what ways am I comfortable with my sexuality? Do I enjoy sex? If I am having sexual difficulties, do I know why? Have I sought professional help?

15. Do I have a God of love or a God of fear in my life? How can I change my attitude toward my Higher Power?

16. Do I take on responsibilities that are not mine? Why or why not?

17. Do I do for others what they can do for themselves? Why?

18. Do I feel responsible for someone else's learning, marriage, or sobriety? How?

In Step Four we have begun the journey to self-trust through self-knowledge. As we continue the journey through the Steps, we gain trust in ourselves, our Higher Power, in other people, and in life. The path to recovery using the Twelve Steps—one Step at a time—continues. Before taking the next Step, congratulate yourself, call your Sponsor, and share at your next home group meeting the excitement and relief you feel from doing your own personal Fourth Step.

Working Step Five

Admitted to God, to ourselves and to another human being the exact nature of our wrongs.

AS WE prepare to admit our faults, we can begin by asking ourselves the following questions or use them for a group discussion.

1. If I have completed my Fourth Step inventory, how do I feel about sharing details of my past with another person?

2. In what areas of my past am I willing to be completely honest?

3. What are some of the advantages I might get from admitting my faults?

4. Do I understand the healing relief that honestly admitting my faults can bring?

5. What expectations do I have about how I should feel or what I should experience when I admit my faults?

6. Am I ready to let these expectations go and allow the God of my understanding to determine the best results for me? How do I know?

7. If I do not feel ready to do this Step, do I need to do more work on Steps One through Four?

8. Would I be willing to group my inventory into things I could admit, things I might admit, and things I think, "No way! I'll never be able to do that," and then start with the "could" list?

9. Am I afraid to admit my faults to my Higher Power? Why?

10. Who in the program could I call to discuss my fears about God?

11. Could I make a list of my fears and turn them over? What are my fears?

12. How can admitting my faults to the God of my understanding help me?

13. Can I concede that I am not perfect? How can I quit trying to be?

14. How do I try to excuse myself from harms I may have done?

15. With whom will I share my Fifth Step? What qualities make me choose this person? Do I trust him or her?

16. Do I have any of those qualities myself? Did I list them under my assets?

17. What may block me from trusting someone with my truth? Can I share these fears with another person?

18. How does my desire to be perfect block me from believing someone could love me unconditionally, even after hearing my Fifth Step?

19. How can telling someone else the exact nature of my wrongs enhance my ability to see myself?

20. How have I isolated myself? Do I believe that sharing with another person can lead to relief from isolation?

21. What is the one thing I don't want to tell another person? Can I start there?

22. Can being honest and admitting a mistake have positive consequences? What are they?

23. Can I remember when another person admitted a fault or mistake to me and I understood and didn't judge?

24. In doing this Fifth Step, what have I learned about the exact nature of my wrongs?

25. What have I learned about fear? Honesty? Trust? Acceptance?

26. How did I feel after sharing with God? Admitting to myself? Sharing with another person?

27. What, if anything, have I left out? If I have completed Step Five, what am I feeling? Is anything different? Better?

Working Step Six

Were entirely ready to have God remove all these defects of character.

THE FOLLOWING questions may generate thought and discussion on Step Six.

1. Have I completed working the first five Steps to the best of my ability? Am I willing to go back and look at them if I feel overwhelmed in working this Step?

2. What have I learned from my Sponsor or another Al-Anon friend on how they worked Step Six?

3. As a result of working Step Five, am I grateful that there is a Step Six to work?

4. Do I clearly understand the concept of readiness?

5. How do I know if I am ready?

6. If I am not entirely ready, how might I turn these fears over to the God of my understanding?

7. What fears block me from being entirely ready?

8. Can I ask God for the willingness to be ready?

9. In what ways do I trust the God of my understanding in working this Step?

10. Am I willing to let go of all my defects of character? Why or why not?

11. Which ones would I prefer to hold on to? What advantages do I see to holding on to them?

12. Which defects of character also contained assets?

13. What does "have God remove all of my defects of character" mean to me?

14. How do I trust and feel confident that my Higher Power is there for me?

15. Do I understand why this Step speaks only of my own relationship with God? What does this mean to me?

16. How am I grateful that I now know the God of my understanding?

17. Can I make a commitment to share in an Al-Anon meeting how I worked this Step?

18. How have I encouraged those I sponsor to work this Step?

19. Will I consider chairing a meeting or workshop on the power of this Step?

20. What evidence do I see in my life today of my Higher Power's willingness to help me improve my behavior? How can I do my part?

21. Do I make demands on God, praying for a specific result rather than trusting God to know which defect is most important to remove?

22. How can I look at all these characteristics from a fresh point of view today?

23. Other than "Let Go and Let God" what other Al-Anon slogans or tools can help me with this Step?

Working Step Seven

Humbly asked Him to remove our shortcomings.

IN WORKING Step Seven, some of us pray for the willingness to release our shortcomings and then trust that God will take them from us. Questions for thought and discussion:

1. What does humility mean to me? List people I know who possess this trait.

2. How am I humble? What can help me be more so?

3. What old behaviors get in the way of my being humble?

4. What defects am I ready to have removed?

5. Do I believe that my Higher Power can rid me of my defects? How do I know this?

6. Am I ready to ask God to remove my defects?

7. How do I humbly ask God to take my shortcomings?

8. Which shortcoming is causing me the most trouble right now? What benefits do I get from it? What problems does it cause?

9. How can I treat myself with compassion in my recovery and ask for the willingness to keep trying?

10. Do I have a Sponsor? If I don't have one, how can I ask someone to help me?

11. What character defects will I have to overcome to allow myself to turn to a Sponsor for help?

12. What can I do to cooperate with my Higher Power in removing my shortcomings?

13. What positive changes can I make in myself?

14. What positive trait do I want to develop or substitute for a trait I want to eliminate?

15. What can I do this week to practice a positive trait?

16. Have I had any fears removed from my life? Which ones?

17. What negative behaviors or traits are lessening or have been removed?

18. What slogan could remind me to find a substitute for a negative behavior I wish to release?

19. Am I able to see challenges as opportunities to practice new character traits?

20. Am I able to laugh fondly at my mistakes and not be devastated when I am not perfect? Can I love and celebrate my humanness while working for balance?

21. As I turn my defects over to God, are new shortcomings coming to light? If so, can I continue to ask God for help?

22. As I work Step Seven, do I see a change in my relationship with my Higher Power?

Working Step Eight

Made a list of all persons we had harmed and became willing to make amends to them all

AL-ANON MEMBERS have offered various approaches to this Step. The following questions may provide further guidance.

1. Have I resisted making a list? If so, why?

2. Did I use my Fourth Step as a tool in preparing my list? How?

3. Did I consult with my Sponsor or others in Al-Anon on how they made their list? What suggestions did they make? How can I learn from them?

4. Am I willing to make amends? If no, why not? If yes, am I willing to write about my experience?

5. How have I used rationalization or justification to block me from becoming willing?

6. Do I understand that willingness is different than making the actual amends? Describe the differences.

7. Have I considered praying for the willingness to become willing? How patient am I in allowing myself to grow into willingness for making difficult amends?

8. How willing am I to be completely honest?

9. Which people on my list am I willing to contact first? Why?

10. Have I included myself on my list? Why or why not?

11. How does the God of my understanding play a role in this Step?

12. Can I share with my group my thoughts, feelings, and challenges with this Step?

13. How can I encourage those I sponsor to begin working this Step based on my own personal experiences?

14. As I work Step Eight, how do I envision it helping me in my relationship with the alcoholics in my life? My coworkers or friends? My extended family?

15. In reviewing my list, is there a pattern reflecting new defects in my character? Can I see how those defects harmed those on my list? Is this a pattern I identified in working Steps Five and Six?

16. Do I recognize when my minding someone else's business may have harmed them or others? Am I willing to recognize the need for my amends?

Working Step Nine

Made direct amends to such people wherever possible, except when to do so would injure them or others.

HERE ARE some questions to ask ourselves or discuss in our groups to assist us in proceeding with making our amends.

1. Which people on my list do I need to make direct amends to first? What's stopping me?

2. How can I plan what I am going to say in my direct amends to be clear and concise and to avoid blaming any other person?

3. What doubts do I have about my amends injuring someone? Can I discuss these doubts with my Sponsor? Pray to be guided? Write about them?

4. What are my motives for making amends? Am I willing to accept the outcome, whatever it may be?

5. What is the difference between an apology and making amends? Which amends will be best done by changes in my behavior?

6. How can I be sure I am not just ducking an embarrassing situation?

7. What amends am I putting off? Why?

8. Do I have any amends to make that could result in serious consequences for my family, like loss of employment or a prison term? How can I use my Sponsor or trusted friend to help me sort these out?

9. Who on my amends list will never be available for direct amends? Can I make amends in another way? Can I do something for another person?

10. What harm have I done to my children or immediate family? Can I make some amends by respecting them now as adults?

11. Am I willing to pray to become willing to make amends in the future?

12. How can I forgive myself for all the difficulties I've caused myself? What can I do this week to begin my amends to myself?

13. Could I write an amends letter to myself?

14. When I have finished this action Step, what can I do to celebrate? Have I remembered to appreciate and reward my good deeds? The good deeds of others?

Working Step Ten

Continued to take personal inventory and when we were wrong promptly admitted it.

SOME MEMBERS find it useful to make a chart that includes a list of typical personal weaknesses and strengths that can be checked off before going to bed. A mental review of the day chronologically or taking note of any event that produced uncomfortable feelings also works. The following questions may help develop the habit of continual inventory.

1. What is the purpose of Step Ten?

2. How do I feel about continuing to take a personal inventory?

3. What means of taking daily inventory is comfortable for me?

4. What will help me continue to apply program tools when life gets rough?

5. How can I be patient with myself if I feel I'm not growing fast enough?

6. When might I need to take a spot-check?

7. What can I do with my spot-check inventory?

8. In a daily inventory, I can ask myself:

9. What were the major events of the day?

10. What feelings did I experience?

11. How did I deal with them?

12. Did I get myself involved in any situation today I had no business being in?

13. What can help me to accept myself as I make mistakes again and again?

14. Did fear or faith rule my actions today?

15. How can I admit my wrongs despite my pride and fear that it will be used against me?

16. Am I at fault for trying for peace at any price? What are my motives?

17. How do I know when to make amends and when not to?

18. What positive traits did I exhibit today?

19. What negative traits did I exhibit today?

20. How did I try to fix anyone today?

21. How can I "Let Go and Let God"?

22. Did I abandon my own needs today? How?

23. Have I been too accommodating, saying "yes" when I wanted to say "no"?

24. Was I afraid of an authority figure? Of anyone? Why or why not?

25. What small things can I do to practice standing up for myself?

26. How did I take on anyone else's responsibility today?

27. What am I afraid will happen if I don't take on extra responsibility?

28. If I was wrong, did I promptly admit it?

29. What can I do to take good care of myself today?

30. Is there something that I need to take a longer look at? What is it?

31. Have I done something difficult or particularly well today? How can I appreciate myself for it?

32. How could sharing my daily Tenth Step Inventory with another person, such as my Sponsor, help me?

33. What characteristics show up most often in my inventory?

34. Why do I resist having them removed?

35. After practicing the Tenth Step, how have my feelings about it changed?

Working Step Eleven

Sought through prayer and meditation to improve our conscious contact with God as we understood Him, praying only for knowledge of His will for us and the power to carry that out.

1. How do I define the difference between prayer and meditation? Can I talk to my Sponsor, another Al-Anon friend, or someone I am sponsoring about the difference?

2. Am I willing to try prayer and meditation today?

3. What can I do to add prayer and meditation to my life today?

4. Do I have a special time and place to pray and meditate? What can I do to create one?

5. How have I sought to improve my conscious contact? Have I sought out help from my group? My Sponsor? Anyone else in Al-Anon?

6. What personal spiritual experiences can I draw on to help me improve my conscious contact with a Higher Power?

7. What does it mean to me to pray only for God's will and not my own? How can I distinguish between God's will and my self-will?

8. How have I been mistaken about God's will? How has my self-will caused me difficulties?

9. How am I willing to be guided today?

10. Is something blocking me in this Step today? What is it? What Steps can I review to help me feel connected again?

11. What do I need to have the power to carry out God's will for me? Have I asked God for that power?

Working Step Twelve

Having had a spiritual awakening as the results of these steps, we tried to carry this message to others, and to practice these principles in all our affairs.

THERE ARE many spiritual awakenings and many ways to carry the message. Al-Anon members offer these ideas and questions to help us explore the meaning of the Twelfth Step.

1. Have I experienced a spiritual awakening(s)? Describe.

2. In what ways do I downplay my spiritual growth? What can help me to acknowledge it?

3. What have I received from Al-Anon that I would most like to share?

4. What are the different ways I can carry this message to others?

5. Did I see a friendly face early in my recovery? What can I do to be a friendly face to someone else?

6. What is the difference between carrying the message and giving advice?

7. When trying to carry the message, what have I experienced?

8. How can I recognize a cry for help without meddling in other people's affair?

9. How can I best carry the message to my family members, especially those who resist the ideas?

10. How can I practice these principles in my financial affairs? Is my job merely a means of earning money or an opportunity to practice my recovery?

11. What does the Twelfth Step say to me about Al-Anon service work?

12. What part has service to Al-Anon played in my recovery?

13. What would change if I viewed service as my goal in every area of my life?

14. What are "these principles"?

15. How can I apply them in my daily life?

16. In what areas of my life do I need to start practicing these principles? What can I do this week to make a beginning?

17. How am I living the message of the program?

18. How am I a good example of Al-Anon recovery?

Twelve Traditions

THE TRADITIONS that follow bind us together in unity. They guide the groups in their relations with other groups, with A.A. and the outside world. They recommend group attitudes toward leadership, membership, money, property, public relations, and anonymity.

The Traditions evolved from the experience of A.A. groups in trying to solve their problems of living and working together. Al-Anon adopted these group guidelines and over the years has found them sound and wise. Although they are only suggestions, Al-Anon's unity and perhaps even its survival are dependent on adherence to these principles.

1. Our common welfare should come first; personal progress for the greatest number depends upon unity.

2. For our group purpose there is but one authority—a loving God as He may express Himself in our group conscience. Our leaders are but trusted servants—they do not govern.

3. The relatives of alcoholics, when gathered together for mutual aid, may call themselves an Al-Anon Family Group, provided that, as a group, they have no other affiliation. The only requirement for membership is that there be a problem of alcoholism in a relative or friend.

4. Each group should be autonomous, except in matters affecting another group or Al-Anon or AA as a whole.

5. Each Al-Anon Family Group has but one purpose: to help families of alcoholics. We do this by practicing the Twelve Steps of AA *ourselves*, by encouraging and understanding our alcoholic relatives, and by welcoming and giving comfort to families of alcoholics.

6. Our Family Groups ought never endorse, finance or lend our name to any outside enterprise, lest problems of money, property and prestige divert us from our primary spiritual aim. Although a separate entity, we should always co-operate with Alcoholics Anonymous.

7. Every group ought to be fully self-supporting, declining outside contributions.

8. Al-Anon Twelfth Step work should remain forever non-professional, but our service centers may employ special workers.

9. Our groups, as such, ought never be organized; but we may create service boards or committees directly responsible to those they serve.

10. The Al-Anon Family Groups have no opinion on outside issues; hence our name ought never be drawn into public controversy.

11. Our public relations policy is based on attraction rather than promotion; we need always maintain personal anonymity at the level of press, radio, films, and TV. We need guard with special care the anonymity of all AA members.

12. Anonymity is the spiritual foundation of all our Traditions, ever reminding us to place principles above personalities.

Working Tradition One

Our common welfare should come first; personal progress for the greatest number depends upon unity.

1. How can I apply this Tradition to my everyday life?

2. How do I use this Tradition in my meeting?

3. How does this Tradition give me the right to offer my opinion? How can I do this without dominating or having to "win"?

4. What does "common welfare" mean to me? My group? In other areas of service work within Al-Anon?

5. What does "unity" mean to me? My group? In other areas of service work within Al-Anon?

6. Do I consider myself to be open minded? Always?

7. Am I willing to respect others' views? How?

8. Am I willing to accept and appreciate what others are able to give?

9. Am I expressing myself for unity or for manipulation and control?

10. How do I keep Al-Anon unity in mind when expressing my opinion?

11. How am I flexible?

12. Am I bringing anything positive to this group? My family? My personal relationships?

13. Do endless sharings at meetings hinder the unity of the group? If so, how can this be handled?

14. What other ways do groups suffer when members dominate meetings?

15. How can I be a part of the solution of my group's problems not a part of the problem?

16. Am I giving with love? How?

17. Do I listen with love to those I dislike or don't agree with?

18. Am I an informed Al-Anon member, supporting my group, district, Area and World Service Office in all of their affairs? How can I become informed?

19. Do I welcome newcomers in the same manner as my long-time Al-Anon friends? Am I willing to change?

20. When I share, am I honest in sharing the good as well as the bad? Do I listen to the wisdom of longtime members? My Sponsor?

21. Do I understand that there are no rules, but that there are suggested guidelines created for the common welfare of Al-Anon groups worldwide? How will this change my participation in Al-Anon? In my family? With others?

Working Tradition Two

For our group purpose there is but one authority—a loving God as He may express Himself in our group conscience. Our leaders are but trusted servants—they do not govern.

1. Am I willing to take time to discuss all points of view before reaching a decision? Does my need to be right get in the way? How?

2. How do I participate in my group's business?

3. Do I listen to others in group discussion with an open mind?

4. What am I willing to do for service work?

5. Does my group practice rotation of leadership positions?

6. What can I do to contribute to service in my group and elsewhere?

7. Has my group ever taken a group conscience?

8. Does everyone in our group participate in the group conscience process?

9. What can I do if one member starts to dominate a group?

10. What is the difference between Al-Anon leadership and governing?

11. How am I willing to support the group conscience even if I don't agree with it?

12. Am I contributing to the health of my group? How?

13. Do I bring my concerns to group level with love? How?

14. How am I a leader and a trusted servant? How can I be a leader without "being in charge"?

15. Am I being honest with myself and others?

16. Am I trying to control? Convince others that I am right?

17. Do I give up my responsibilities and then blame others if things go wrong?

18. Am I listening for God's words in others? What do I hear?

Working Tradition Three

The relatives of alcoholics, when gathered together for mutual aid, may call themselves an Al-Anon Family Group, provided that, as a group, they have no other affiliation. The only requirement for membership is that there be a problem of alcoholism in a relative or friend.

1. Do I give each newcomer a warm and loving welcome?

2. Do I welcome all who attend our meeting even if they are different from me in age? Sex? Sexual orientation? Socioeconomic background? How can my group be more welcoming of those who are different from us?

3. Are there members to whom I have not reached out?

4. Do I treat each member and potential member with unconditional love?

5. How does my group encourage all members to share? Do I encourage all members to share?

6. How can my group welcome members of other programs and maintain our Al-Anon focus? What can I do to make them welcome?

7. Have I alienated anyone that might have needed Al-Anon because I thought another meeting might be better for them?

8. How can I help my group remain open to new ideas while assuring that we not affiliate with any other cause or group?

9. Do I leave my other affiliations and interests outside the doors of Al-Anon?

10. Am I being understanding and encouraging?

11. How can I treat others with acceptance, tolerance and love?

12. Am I accepting myself and others as we are? How?

13. How can I apply Tradition Three to other areas of my life?

Working Tradition Four

Each group should be autonomous, except in matters affecting another group or Al-Anon or AA as a whole.

1. How am I taking responsibility for my actions and thoughts? Is my group taking responsibility for its actions and thoughts? How?

2. How am I allowing others the freedom to take responsibility for their own actions and thoughts?

3. Am I accepting the consequences of my actions gracefully? Am I allowing others the same opportunity?

4. Am I self-serving and selfish in the name of autonomy, or am I truly self-caring, asking for my Higher Power's guidance?

5. How does my group consider the impact of its decisions on Al-Anon and Alateen as a whole? Has the group considered Lone Members, inmates, groups throughout the world? A.A.? Newcomers? Longtime members?

6. What were my feelings as a new member? Did I feel welcomed? Can I share my thoughts with my group? Others?

7. Do I remember Al-Anon's primary purpose—to help families and friends of alcoholics—in my service activities? How does this affect my actions?

8. Am I dogmatic in my reasoning, or am I flexible in the interpretation of the suggested guidelines? How can I be more flexible?

9. When visiting a new group, do I feel irritated if it's not just like my home group? Do I want to straighten them out? What can I learn from visiting other groups?

10. In my personal life, how can I apply this Tradition to my family? Are we autonomous? Do our actions affect other families? Our community?

11. Tradition Four asks us to be obedient to the unenforceable. What does this mean to me?

Working Tradition Five

Each Al-Anon Family Group has but one purpose: to help families of alcoholics. We do this by practicing the Twelve Steps of AA ourselves, by encouraging and understanding our alcoholic relatives, and by welcoming and giving comfort to families of alcoholics.

1. How do I describe our primary purpose in a meeting? To newcomers?

2. Do I put my recovery first, ahead of others' needs? When? How?

3. Do I realize that welcoming and giving comfort is not limited to newcomers? Why?

4. Am I welcoming to all newcomers, no matter what their problems? How can I guide them to focus on the alcohol-related aspect of those problems?

5. How can I be more "newcomer friendly"?

6. How do I welcome members who have been in the program awhile or those who have returned after a long absence?

7. How might my group give newcomers individual attention?

8. Do I ever call newcomers or someone who has been missing from our meeting?

9. As a group, how do we use the Steps and Traditions to help families of alcoholics?

10. What can we as a group do to make our fellowship known to people outside Al-Anon?

11. How can I help others understand that alcoholism is a disease?

12. What does comfort mean to me? How can I extend that to another person?

13. What does encouraging the alcoholic mean to me? How might I react differently if the diseased person I love had diabetes or cancer?

Working Tradition Six

Our Family Groups ought never endorse, finance or lend our name to any outside enterprise, lest problems of money, property and prestige divert us from our primary spiritual aim. Although a separate entity, we should always co-operate with Alcoholics Anonymous.

1. Why do we not "endorse, finance or lend our name to any outside enterprise"? How is this principle used in our business meetings?

2. Has my group ever had problems with money or property? How were these problems resolved?

3. Have I or any member of my group allowed prestige to divert us from our primary spiritual aim? When? Why? What did we change?

4. How does my group cooperate with A.A.? When?

5. In planning a group fund-raising activity, has my group considered this Tradition?

6. Does my group have CAL prominently displayed? Do I use CAL in my personal recovery?

7. Does my group sell or promote outside literature? How does this violate Tradition Six? Do I have the courage to discuss the use of literature at a meeting?

8. How do I consider cooperation with A.A. in my service work?

9. Why should group funds support only Al-Anon programs?

10. Has our group phone list ever been used for promotional purposes? How?

11. How can I discourage members, without embarrassing them, from bringing outside enterprises into our meetings?

12. Am I allowing material or financial concerns to gain priority over my personal spiritual needs and serenity?

13. Am I allowing personal problems or success to overwhelm me? Am I letting them get in the way of how I treat others?

14. How can I apply our slogan, "Live and Let Live" to this Tradition?

15. How can I apply our slogan, "Let Go and Let God"?

16. How do I help my group to fulfill our primary spiritual aim?

17. When participating at an A.A. Convention or roundup, do Al-Anon members have Al-Anon logos or the name Al-Anon on their badges?

Working Tradition Seven

Every group ought to be fully self-supporting, declining outside contributions.

1. What does fully self-supporting mean to me?

2. How do I support my group?

3. What can I do this week to contribute to my own support and to that of my group?

4. Do I consider costs and what my group needs when I decide how much to contribute, or do I just keep tossing a dollar into the basket? Can I put a little more in the basket on behalf of the new person who can't?

5. Do I personally contribute to the World Service Office quarterly appeal?

6. If members of my group do not understand the quarterly appeal, am I willing to explain its purpose to them?

7. Does my group pay a fair rate for rent, copying, refreshments, and does it have enough literature?

8. Do I encourage business meetings for my group?

9. In what ways, other than financial, do I support my group?

10. What benefits have I received when I have volunteered?

11. How often do we rotate service positions? Do we expect a few people to hold up the rest of us?

12. What could I do to encourage less active members to become involved? Am I as active as I would like to be?

13. Do we ever expect members in service positions to personally purchase coffee or to print lists at their offices?

14. Do I support our service boards, such as district, Information Services, Literature Distribution Center, Intergroup, Area, WSO? How? With money or time?

15. What does my group do to support our service boards?

16. How do we support our district?

17. How do we support our Area?

18. How do we support the WSO?

19. Do we contribute to the large group conscience by sending our Group Representative (GR) as our voice and vote at district or Area meetings?

20. What benefits do we get from being part of the worldwide fellowship?

21. Do I subscribe to The Forum? Do I purchase gift subscriptions?

22. Does my group have a Group Treasurer? Does the Treasurer give regular reports?

23. Has my group been prudent enough to establish an ample, though not excessive, reserve, or are we stockpiling moneys for no specific reason?

24. Do I understand the spiritual aspects of contributing?

25. Is my self-worth based on how much I'm needed by others?

26. Am I afraid of letting go?

27. Do I realize I can't have the respect of others if I can't stand on my own two feet?

28. Do I contribute to my own well-being? Am I fully self-supporting? Am I prepared to remain so?

29. Can I accept and express my own feelings without feeling wrong or justifying them to others?

30. Do I take responsibility for my own feelings or do I blame them on the actions of others?

31. Is my happiness circumstance-dependent, or am I looking to myself for fulfillment? Explain.

Working Tradition Eight

Al-Anon Twelfth Step work should remain forever non-professional, but our service centers may employ special workers.

1. Do I willingly share my experience, strength, and hope with those who are suffering from the family disease of alcoholism?

2. Do I ever have a tendency to be a know-it-all?

3. How can I share with others without trying to fix them?

4. At meetings do I speak as an expert or as a fellow member?

5. Do I ever regard other members as experts, perhaps because they are longtime members, very charismatic, or professionals outside of Al-Anon?

6. Do I ever hold back from sharing because I feel I don't know as much as others?

7. What is the difference between Twelfth Step work and being a special worker?

8. Am I committed to paying our special workers a fair wage, or do I expect them to give a lot for free because they are Al-Anon members?

9. Do I understand what our local and WSO special workers do?

10. Do I feel the need to look good or to be a perfect model of recovery? Does that stop me from being humble enough to get the help I need?

11. Is someone else's opinion more important than my own? Why?

12. Am I ever Mr. or Ms. Al-Anon?

13. Am I ever judgmental?

14. Do I take others' inventories? Is this ever appropriate?

Working Tradition Nine

Our groups, as such, ought never be organized; but we may create service boards or committees directly responsible to those they serve.

1. How often does my group rotate our leadership positions? Is everyone encouraged to participate?

2. Does our group have unnecessary extra rules for its servants or members?

3. Do I try to control my group by organizing it? Why?

4. How flexible am I? How flexible is my group? How might we encourage flexibility at our meetings without creating chaos?

5. How do I resist suggestions for changes in structure? Why?

6. How does my group support our service boards and committees (Literature Distribution Center, Information Service, Public Outreach, etc.)?

7. How do I support our service boards and committees? Do I donate money? Do I volunteer?

8. How can I benefit from being a trusted servant?

9. How have I gained any patience or humility by serving the group?

10. How do I treat those who serve us? Do I appreciate them and support them, or criticize and second guess them?

11. How do I acknowledge my trusted servants' need to report back to my group and support them?

12. Has my group invited any district or Area trusted servants to our meeting to share their experiences?

13. When my service term is over, have I encouraged new servants by passing on my records and experiences? Have I ever tried to interfere with a trusted servant's way of doing things, or do I practice "Let Go and Let God"?

14. Has my group discussed our role in the entire Al-Anon structure? Do we tend to think that the only thing that matters is our home group?

15. What can we do to connect with the worldwide fellowship that will enhance our own recovery?

16. Have I ever considered that service rotation keeps me humble?

17. How am I taking on my share of responsibilities?

18. How am I taking responsibility for my own actions?

19. Do I speak up when others' actions are unacceptable, or am I so fearful of confrontation that I am willing to have peace at any price—even the loss of my own serenity?

20. How am I putting my abilities to their best use?

21. Am I taking on more than I can handle?

22. Do I understand Al-Anon's service structure?

23. Have I ever considered being a Service Sponsor?

Working Tradition Ten

The Al-Anon Family Groups have no opinion on outside issues; hence our name ought never be drawn into public controversy.

1. How do I concentrate on our common bonds rather than on our differences?

2. Do I remember that there is no official Al-Anon opinion?

3. Have I ever asked my Al-Anon group to further a cause or business venture?

4. If someone does bring up what I think is an outside issue, how can I gently bring discussion back to our Al-Anon approach?

5. Have I called my Sponsor to air out my anger or resentment?

6. How do I let myself react to emotions rather than thinking about what I want to say and how I want to say it?

7. Can I find ways to say what I mean without being mean when I say it? How?

8. Am I defensive because someone doesn't agree with me? How do I respond?

9. Even though I have a right to my feelings and opinions, can I admit that I am sorry for letting my anger control my emotions?

10. Do I ever give the impression that there is an Al-Anon opinion on a subject?

11. What would Al-Anon be like without this Tradition?

12. How can I use this Tradition in my personal life?

Working Tradition Eleven

Our public relations policy is based on attraction rather than promotion; we need always maintain personal anonymity at the level of press, radio, films, and TV. We need guard with special care the anonymity of all AA members.

1. What can my group do to inform people of its existence?

2. What can I do as an individual?

3. Am I careful to keep the confidences of other members?

4. How do I support our Information Services?

5. When I talk to the media or write about Al-Anon, do I request that my face and name be left out of the story?

6. When I write about myself and use my name, do I avoid implying that I am a member of Al-Anon?

7. How can I talk about my recovery without revealing the identity of the alcoholics in my life?

8. How can I share Al-Anon with friends and colleagues who might be interested while keeping the spirit of anonymity alive?

9. Am I attracting others to my new way of life or trying to convince them to change? How?

10. Am I the man or woman I want to be? Why or why not?

11. Do I ever over-promote Al-Anon, making it unattractive?

12. How am I practicing the Steps and Traditions in all phases of my life?

13. How am I grateful for the people in my life?

14. Am I trying to force someone into living the way I think is right? How?

15. What is the value of anonymity to me?

16. What does it mean to me to carry the message while remaining personally anonymous at the public level?

17. Is my recovery attractive to others?

Working Tradition Twelve

Anonymity is the spiritual foundation of all our Traditions, ever reminding us to place principles above personalities.

1. Do I practice this Tradition in all of my affairs? How?

2. Am I able to listen to others with an open mind, or am I discounting them because they are not agreeing with me?

3. Do I understand the spiritual foundation of my personal anonymity? My group's? My Area's?

4. Am I able to see the good in others or just notice their faults?

5. How do I remember not to identify anyone or tell an identifiable story even if I'm speaking to a group member?

6. What is the relationship between anonymity and confidentiality?

7. Do I put anyone in our group on a pedestal, expecting more of them than I do of myself?

8. If a well-known member of my community comes into my group, do I resist letting people know I have seen them in Al-Anon?

9. How do I let Al-Anon be known without breaking anyone's anonymity?

10. What does it mean to understand that it is up to each of us to decide just how anonymous we want to be?

11. Do I ever use Al-Anon to promote my personal agenda? Products? Ideologies?

12. Do I respect Al-Anon's trusted servants and thank them for their service?

13. Is Al-Anon a secret in my community?

14. How does Tradition Twelve relate to Tradition Ten? To Tradition Eleven?

15. When I meet people I know from Al-Anon outside of a meeting, how can I acknowledge them while protecting their anonymity?

16. How does my group inform all members about our principle of anonymity? Do we do this on a regular basis?

17. How does this Tradition impact Al-Anon's primary purpose?

18. What is the importance of my membership in the Al-Anon fellowship to the worldwide fellowship?

19. How has study of the Traditions improved my understanding of my role in my group?

20. How has study of the Traditions improved my understanding of my group's role in our district? In our Area? In worldwide Al-Anon?

21. How can I apply the Traditions to my personal life? To my work life?

Twelve Concepts of Service

THE TWELVE Steps and Traditions are guides for personal growth and group unity. The Twelve Concepts are guides for service. They show how Twelfth Step work can be done on a broad scale and how members of a World Service Office can relate to each other and to the groups, through a World Service Conference, to spread Al-Anon's message worldwide.

1. The ultimate responsibility and authority for Al-Anon world services belongs to the Al-Anon groups.

2. The Al-Anon Family Groups have delegated complete administrative and operational authority to their Conference and its service arms.

3. The right of decision makes effective leadership possible.

4. Participation is the key to harmony.

5. The rights of appeal and petition protect minorities and insure that they be heard.

6. The Conference acknowledges the primary administrative responsibility of the Trustees.

7. The Trustees have legal rights while the rights of the Conference are traditional.

8. The Board of Trustees delegates full authority for routine management of Al-Anon Headquarters to its executive committees.

9. Good personal leadership at all service levels in a necessity. In the field of world service the Board of Trustees assumes the primary leadership.

10. Service responsibility is balanced by carefully defined service authority and double-headed management is avoided.

11. The World Service Office is composed of selected committees, executives and staff members.

12. The spiritual foundation for Al-Anon's world services is contained in the General Warranties of the Conference, Article 12 of the Charter.

GENERAL WARRANTIES OF THE CONFERENCE

IN ALL proceedings the World Service Conference of Al-Anon shall observe the spirit of the Traditions:

1. that only sufficient operating funds, including an ample reserve, be its prudent financial principle;

2. that no Conference member shall be placed in unqualified authority over the members;

3. that all decisions be reached by discussion vote and whenever possible by unanimity;

4. that no Conference action ever be personally punitive or an incitement to public controversy;

5. that though the Conference serves Al-Anon it shall never perform any act of government; and that like the fellowship of Al-Anon Family Groups which it serves, it shall always remain democratic in thought and action.

Working Concept One

The ultimate responsibility and authority for Al-Anon world services belongs to the Al-Anon groups.

1. What does Al-Anon world service do for us?

2. Does my group take responsibility for supporting Al-Anon world services? In what ways?

3. Do we support our district? Area? WSO?

4. Do we participate in district and Assembly meetings? How?

5. How do we keep ourselves informed?

6. Does information from the Delegate get passed on to the District Representative? Group Representative? Group?

7. Do I trust in the process?

8. How well do I accept decisions of my district? My Area Assembly? The World Service Conference?

9. Do we hold regular business meetings?

10. Do we welcome newcomers?

11. For what part of my life am I ultimately responsible? What responsibilities might I share or delegate?

12. How do I contribute to the group conscience?

13. Referring to Tradition Two and Concept One, can I accept and support the group conscience when I don't agree with the outcome?

14. Do I express my gratitude for service work?

Working Concept Two

The Al-Anon Family Groups have delegated complete administrative and operational authority to their Conference and its service arms.

1. How does my group encourage newer members to become involved in service?

2. Do I attend an Al-Anon meeting that I call my home group?

3. Does my group hold business meetings?

4. Does my group have a Group Representative? Does that trusted servant attend district meetings? Area meetings?

5. Does my group participate in decisions made at Area Assemblies? Do we know who our trusted servants are? Have we asked one of our trusted servants to attend our meetings?

6. Have I ever attended our Area's Delegate report after the World Service Conference (WSC)?

7. Has our group ever sent our Delegate a loving card of support when he/she attends the WSC each year?

8. When our group gets a copy of the annual Conference Summary, do we read and/or discuss it?

9. Do I have a Service Sponsor? Do I know someone I can ask?

10. What service characteristics do I want that others have?

11. Am I willing to be a Service Sponsor?

12. Do I thank our trusted servant for representing us at the district and Area business meetings?

13. Do I understand the function of some of the many service arms?

14. Does my Area invite our Regional Trustee to attend our Assembly on a regular basis?

15. Why is it important to delegate both responsibility and authority in general? In Al-Anon?

16. Am I able to share responsibility? What responsibility? Am I willing to offer my assistance to others?

17. When do I rely on others? Can I ask for help?

18. What responsibilities in my life could I delegate to someone else?

19. Whom can I trust to be reliable?

20. Am I reliable and trustworthy? In what ways?

21. How willing am I to work with others and to consider their ideas? How often do I trust the knowledge and experience of another person? Do I support and encourage others?

22. For what am I responsible?

23. How willing am I to try something new?

Working Concept Three

The right of decision makes effective leadership possible.

1. Do I ever ask someone to do a task and then try to direct the details of how it should be done? If so, how can I change this pattern?

2. What would give me confidence to decide when to take charge of a job and when to consult with those who might be affected?

3. In what ways am I willing to be responsible for the outcome of my decisions?

4. Do we, as a group, trust our trusted servants?

5. What do we need to do to help our trusted servants?

6. Have I shared with my group the process I used as a trusted servant in making an informed decision?

7. Do I use the Al-Anon/Alateen Service Manual as a tool to make my decision? My Service Sponsor? Those who have served before me?

8. What leadership qualities do our leaders possess that I aspire to have?

9. Can I make a decision and be comfortable with it? If not, why not?

Working Concept Four

Participation is the key to harmony.

1. Am I an active participant in Al-Anon? Why or why not?

2. What can I do to participate more fully?

3. What can I do to encourage others to share their opinions freely?

4. Is there a situation in my life today where those concerned do not participate equally in all decisions?

5. What can I do to make such situations more harmonious?

6. Am I willing to hear all that others may share?

7. How am I willing to learn more about myself as I share with others?

8. Am I willing to risk discovering that I have more to offer than I thought?

9. Can I trust that there is more than one good or right way to do something? Give examples.

10. In what areas of my life can I apply Concept Four? What might the results be?

Working Concept Five
The rights of appeal and petition protect minorities and insure that they be heard.

1. When I am in the minority, how willing am I to speak up?

2. What would make me more willing?

3. How do I encourage others to voice their opinions?

4. Do I truly listen to those with whom I disagree?

5. How can I extend consideration to those with whom I disagree?

6. How can I keep an open mind to different ideas?

7. What are the benefits of encouraging minority reports and discussing issues even when the majority agrees? What disadvantages keep us from doing it?

8. How willing am I to listen to Al-Anon?

9. How willing am I to listen to my family?

10. How willing am I to listen at work?

Working Concept Six

The Conference acknowledges the primary administrative responsibility of the Trustees.

1. Do I know what Region my Area is located in?

2. Do I know who my Regional Trustee is?

3. What administrative responsibilities are required of my group in order to continue operating?

4. Does my group delegate these administrative responsibilities? To whom?

5. Does my group hold business meetings on a regular basis?

6. Does my group expect the Treasurer to give regular reports on our income and expenses?

7. How is this Concept a spiritual principle?

8. How can I apply this Concept to my work life?

9. How can I apply this Concept to my family life?

10. How does this Concept relate to Concept Three and Al-Anon's "links of service"?

Working Concept Seven

The Trustees have legal rights while the rights of the Conference are traditional.

1. What does "legal rights" mean to me?

2. What are "traditional rights" in my group? Who holds "legal rights"?

3. What are the legal responsibilities of the members of our group? The members of our district? The members of our Assembly? As an Intergroup or Literature Distribution Center? In other service positions?

4. In what situations in our group might it be advisable for our leaders to say "no" to the will of the group?

5. How can I apply this Concept to my home life?

6. How can I apply this Concept to my work life?

7. Is anything out of balance in my life? If so, what?

8. What can I do to balance my spiritual aims with my practical living situation?

Working Concept Eight

The Board of Trustees delegates full authority for routine management of the Al-Anon Headquarters to its executive committees.

1. What are some of the many routine functions performed by our WSO employees to fulfill our primary purpose?

2. What are the management tasks in my group? My district? My Area?

3. How are these tasks delegated?

4. What are the management tasks in my home life? How are these tasks delegated?

5. What are the management tasks in my work life? How are these tasks delegated?

6. What responsibilities or jobs am I willing to delegate to others?

7. Once I delegate a task, am I willing to trust the results?

8. In what areas of my life have I had difficulty trusting?

9. What are the spiritual principles embodied in this Concept?

Working Concept Nine
Good personal leadership at all service levels is a necessity. In the field of world service the Board of Trustees assumes the primary leadership.

1. What is "good personal leadership"?

2. What are the leadership positions available in my group? In my district? In our local Al-Anon Information Service (AIS) or Intergroup? Our local Literature Distribution Center (LDC)? In our Area? At the World Service Conference (WSC)? At the World Service Office (WSO)?

3. Who assumes the primary leadership in my group? My district? My Area? Our AIS? Our LDC?

4. How can I use Concept Nine as a practical, spiritual yardstick for choosing leaders? Roommates? Employers?

5. What are the differences between leadership and management tasks in my life?

6. In what situations have I served as a leader?

7. What qualities of leadership do I have?

8. Which ones would I like to develop?

9. Am I hesitant to be a leader? Why or why not?

10. What does it mean to have vision? How can I share my vision?

11. Do I have a Service Sponsor?

Working Concept Ten

Service responsibility is balanced by carefully defined service authority and double-headed management is avoided.

1. Is service responsibility carefully defined in my group? In my district? In my Area? At our Al-Anon Information Service (AIS), Intergroup, or Literature Distribution Center (LDC)?

2. What is double-headed management? Why do we want to avoid it?

3. In what ways am I willing to delegate enough authority to carry out the job?

4. Am I involved in any double-headed management?

5. Am I involved in any situations where one person has the responsibility while a different person has the authority?

6. What kind of guidelines and definitions of a project would I find helpful before accepting a responsibility?

7. How do I define guidelines for others?

Working Concept Eleven

The World Service Office is composed of selected committees, executives and staff members.

1. What does our World Service Office (WSO) mean to me?

2. What does our WSO mean to our group? Does my group consider the WSO to be a part of our Al-Anon family?

3. How many Area Coordinators does my Area have with positions similar to those at the WSO?

4. What committees serve my district? Our Al-Anon Information Service or Intergroup? My group?

5. Do I respect the amount of time my group, district, and Area trusted servants commit to Al-Anon service work?

6. Have I shown my appreciation to our trusted servants for all that they do for Al-Anon?

7. If my Area has Al-Anon Information Service staff members, do we pay them fair wages? Are these employees treated with respect? Do we thank them for their efforts?

8. Have I studied this Concept with my Service Sponsor to gain a better understanding of its meaning to my group? Our district? Our Area?

9. Do I consult the Al-Anon/Alateen Service Manual when I'm struggling with a problem? If not, am I willing to study it to find the answers? Have I ever introduced a new Al-Anon member to the Manual for its guidance?

10. Do we value our past trusted servants for their wisdom and seek their continued participation?

11. As a trusted servant, do I share openly by passing on my experience to others?

12. What does this Concept teach me about delegation? About turning things over?

13. How is Concept Eleven applicable to my personal life?

14. How is Concept Eleven applicable to my work life?

Working Concept Twelve

The spiritual foundation for Al-Anon's world services is contained in the General Warranties of the Conference, Article 12 of the Charter.

The General Warranties of the Conference:

In all proceedings the World Service Conference of Al-Anon shall observe the spirit of the Traditions:

1. *that only sufficient operating funds, including an ample reserve, be its prudent financial principle;*

2. *that no Conference member shall be placed in unqualified authority over other members;*

3. *that all decisions be reached by discussion vote and whenever possible by unanimity;*

4. *that no Conference action ever be personally punitive or an incitement to public controversy;*

5. *that though the Conference serves Al-Anon, it shall never perform any act of government; and that like the fellowship of Al-Anon Family Groups which it serves, it shall always remain democratic in thought and action.*

1. How does my group practice financial prudence? My district? My Area?

2. How do I practice prudence in my financial affairs?

3. In what other areas of my life could I practice prudence?

4. What does authority mean to me?

5. Do I ever assume unqualified authority? Does my group allow this?

6. Can I listen to all sides of a discussion before making a decision?

7. What is substantial unanimity in my group? My district? My Area? In my family? My job?

8. Can I keep principles above personalities at all times? Why or why not?

9. Do I like to stir things up? If so, why?

10. Does my group practice democratic thought? My district? My Area?

11. How is my family democratic in thought? In action?

12. Is my workplace democratic in thought and action? How?

13. How has study of the Concepts improved my understanding of my role in my group?

14. How has study of the Concepts improved my understanding of my group's role in our district? In our Area? In worldwide Al-Anon?

15. How can I apply the Concepts to my personal life? To my work life?

Notes

Notes